A Guide to Angelic

Mediumship

JANICE FUCHS, LCSW

The information presented in this book is not intended to replace the services of trained mental health professionals or to be a substitute. The clients presented in this book are a composite of the many clients the author has treated and any identifying information is fictional.

Also by Janice Fuchs:

The Forgotten Friend: A simple guide to a new way of being with YOU (May 10, 2014)

Cover design by Noelle Martin

Dedication

This book is dedicated to my two earth angels ~ my daughters, Emma Rose and Noelle Anne.

Table of Contents

A special message from the angels

The angels want you to know you are in the right place. This guide was handmade and woven with love for you. In each and every teaching and exercise, we blend in our angelic energy so you will experience how loved and worthy you are! We want to tell you that anything you would like to learn and master is possible! We share in your excitement for your passion in angelic mediumship and will help you in all ways.

Love,
Your Angels.

Angelic Mediumship

Hi my name is Janice Mary and I am so excited to talk to you about angelic mediumship. Working with the angels is my passion and I am thrilled to be able to share with you how to connect with the angels to learn the special language of mediumship.

We are all spiritual beings and when we were in spirit, we spoke the language of spirit fluently. Here on earth, we have forgotten this very natural, native tongue. The angels have reminded me how to speak it again so that I can connect with them, spirits and guides in the spiritual realm. We all have the ability to speak and understand this beautiful forgotten language and I am so excited to teach you all that the angels have taught me.

When writing this book, the angels pointed out to me that we still speak this language every night when we go into our dream state. Think about the dreams you have had when you are talking to someone, but their lips were not moving; yet you completely understood what they are saying. You were hearing and feeling what they are talking about through your senses. This is the same way you connect and communicate with an angel or spirit. You see, we haven't completely stopped speaking our native language. We have only forgotten how and when to use it when we are awake. With the angel's help and guidance, I am here to remind and teach you how to speak a language you are already very familiar with.

The Invitation

Invite the angels in to mentor and teach you. Ask your angels to surround you and help you on your new journey of learning mediumship. Feel the angel's presence and love all around you now and on a daily basis, ask an angel to be your personal mentor. This may be an angel you have worked with before or an angel you are drawn to. Many people work with Archangel Michael or Archangel Raphael so you can invite them to be your personal mentor, Archangel Gabriel who is the angel known to help in communication is also a good choice. If you don't resonate with these angels or any of the other archangels you may also consider using your guardian angel. There is no right or wrong way when asking for an angel mentor. The important part is to ask and work on this relationship daily. How do you know your angel will be around you? Ask daily and your angel will make their presence known in very special ways.

Through this guide you will become more aware of how the angels will communicate with you. How this connection begins and how it grows over time. The only requirement of you is to keep tuning into the angels that are always around you loving and supporting your every desire and happiness. In time, your relationship to the angels deepens. Having this beautiful connection and relationship is no longer based on you practicing, you realize you now have a wonderful friend, support and mentor.

An Angelic Journal

It's time to begin your own Angelic Journal. Your journal plays a big role in learning to connect and hear your angels. The angels have so much to teach you. Having a journal is one way to show them your level of commitment; by writing down your thoughts, questions, concerns or fears. The angels will help you work through all your issues and any blocks that you may have when learning. It is helpful to write down any inspired thoughts or ideas that you may receive. Keeping an angel journal is fun and you will be able to track your progress. Make it fun! Go out and get a pretty journal or notebook and decorate it in honor of you and your angel mentor. This is a new relationship that will grow and deepen over time.

Your journal will also help deepen your relationship with your angel mentor. Everyday ask your mentor a question and write down an answer. This helps to begin the dialogue between the two of you. Start with simple questions and feel and listen for their response. Keep a special section in your journal for shower questions, yes in the shower. Get in the habit of asking questions to your angels in the shower. The water helps us to hear the angels and spirit better. Many psychics call the shower the psychic phone booth. I will talk about in more detail in a later chapter. But for now create a special section for shower questions!

Meditate

Learning to connect with spirit means it's time to reconnect with you and your spirit. Meditation helps you develop a new relationship with you, your angels and spirit. If you have never meditated before, start slowly for ten minutes a day. This is a very important part of this guide and is very healthy for you. Meditating not only helps with your relationship with you and spirit but it has the same benefits as exercise.

There are many styles of meditation and I will mention a couple but feel free to research and find a meditation that fits you. An easy basic meditation is to follow your breath. First breathe in slowly for a count of five, hold the breath for a count of four and exhale for a count of six. Do this till you feel nice and relaxed and then just go back to following your natural breathing. Don't worry you can't totally stop your thoughts but you can slow them down. Slowing them down is your goal. When you find yourself thinking just redirect your thoughts back to your breath.

Some other easy meditations are the "candle" and the "phrase" methods.

Light a candle and stare at it for ten minutes. If you start thinking again just bring your attention back to the candle. For the phrase meditation method, use your favorite prayer, phrase or word. Say the prayer over and over or focus on the phrase or one word like "love" or "peace". The object is to relax and slow your thoughts down. In time you will see the benefit and it becomes easy and feels very good. Make it your morning or evening ritual.

Mediating is worth every effort and will teach you how to empty your mind and connect you to your spirit, which is exactly what you are doing when you are speaking to spirit. It also helps you to feel your angels around you and to start feeling the energy of spirit.

Tune in to your frequency

When speaking to the angels or spirit you need to learn to tune out and perceive in a new deep way and then tune back in. Spirit talks through our senses so we have to heighten our senses to use them in a new way. Learning to be in the present moment really helps develop this new way of being.

Next time you go for a walk see everything in a new deep way. Really look at the trees, the leaves, the birds, the sky, look at it like you are looking at it for the first time. Listen to every sound the birds, cars, people, everything. What does today feel like? Is it cold or hot? How would you describe to someone what today feels like? Today feels cold, crisp and clean. Look at everything like you are going to have to describe what you are seeing to someone. This exercise accomplishes a few things. It teaches you to be in the moment, which you have to do when you're doing a reading. It also teaches you to clear out your mind.

When you are speaking to spirit, you are tuning into your senses in a deeper way. To do this we need to develop your clairs.

- Clairvoyance - clear seeing
- Clairaudience - clear hearing

- Clairsentience - clear knowing or feeling
- Clairgustance - clear smelling/tasting

Try to be in the moment and notice everything. When you are eating or taking a shower you can tune in and heighten any daily experience. Do this at least once a day. When you talk with spirit you see, hear, feel, smell and taste in the same way you do in the outer world except when you speak to spirit you bring your clairs inward. Seeing in your minds eye, hearing in your head, feeling from the inside. The best is that you can taste foods with no calories!

Clairvoyance

Clairvoyance means clear seeing: it's fun to practice this clair. Here are some simple yet important exercises to do daily. In your imagination, in your minds eye see an apple. Look at this apple and describe it in detail. The more detail you can see the better. If a spirit gave you an apple it would come in a similar way and you would see it the same way you are now.

The only difference is that when a spirit gives you an apple you aren't bringing the image to yourself spirit does. It floats in seemly out of nowhere when spirit gives it to you. It can take you by surprise when a spirit gives you an image. Why did an apple pop into my mind?

Ask for a symbol now from your angel and see what comes into your mind and write it down in your journal. Now picture your pet in your mind's eye and see all the details of how your pet looks. Just Like when you were focusing during your walk you are doing the same thing but this time instead of looking outside you, you are bringing the images inside.

Now bring a friend in and hold the image of them and look at them closely. What are they wearing and are they standing still or moving? Do they seem happy or sad?

Notice! Use any object or person you know and practice. After you practice rate how hard was this for you on a scale of 1-10. (one being extremely difficult and ten easy to see.) Write this and all your experiences in your journal.

Clairaudience

Clairaudience means clear hearing. Close your eyes and listen to church bells or listen to your favorite song in your mind, this is clairaudience.

I love clairaudience because out of nowhere I will hear something that has nothing to do with what I was thinking. My next question is who is here? Listen to thoughts that come out of nowhere. They can be your angels, guides or spirits. How can you tell? They are thoughts that just float in and aren't in your flow of your thinking. Don't worry they are never bad so if a scary thought pops in it is never the angels, your guides or spirit. There is nothing but love in the spirit realms. I have never experienced anything bad when connecting ever! I think sometimes when a spirit is trying to tell a medium what their personality is like they may misinterpret what they are receiving. Hollywood and some of the psychic shows feed fears that are just not real. In all my years of connecting the only thing I feel is love, a lot of love. Don't buy into the fear. Spirit is love and we are love, the end. Sorry no drama here!

Practice your clairaudience by holding different sounds in your mind. Hear the ocean waves crashing in the beach or a kids laughing and playing. The more you can recall sounds the better. Ask your angels to give you a song that represents you. What is the song? The more you ask questions of your angels and spirit, the more you will hear answers. Ask during meditation and see if you hear anything. Ask questions in the shower like we mentioned earlier.

In time you will be able to really tell the difference between your thoughts and what the angels or spirit is giving you. Make it a habit to ask questions and this will greatly help to develop your clairaudience.

This also helps to deepen your relationship with your angels and mentor. Ask your angel mentor questions and practice hearing your answers. I ask questions about my daughter's test results or how she will do in a horse show she's competing in. I will listen for an answer to practice my clairaudience. Listen closely to your thoughts and pay close attention!

Sometimes hearing is obvious and sometimes it's not. A word will come and go quickly and I could have easily missed it. When you are around your friends ask their spirit people questions and hear an answer. If you sense your friends grandmother is around ask her what did she like to do? Listen for the answer then you can check. Hey did your grandmother like to knit?

Don't worry, no question is too trivial. You are working on connecting and hearing in a very different way than you are used to. Notice what is easier for you to hear? Is hearing a song easy for you or a number? I have an easy time hearing numbers and professions. It seems easy for me to hear teacher, accountant, and mechanic. Ask your angel mentor to give you a friend's name you haven't been in touch with and wait to hear the answer. Rate this clair in your journal on the scale 1-10. Was this your easiest or hardest clair to get?

Clairsentience

Clairsentience means clear knowing and feeling. Have you ever had the experience of just knowing something and you don't know how? You just had a gut feeling about something. Maybe your friend decided to quit her job and you just knew it ahead of time, you had a feeling. Many times we have this experience sometimes daily and we dismiss it. We want to tune into these feelings and notice how often it happens. Try and feel your way through life more. How does this person feel to you? Do they feel warm and engaging or guarded? Pay attention to your intuition and gut feelings as this is part of the language of mediumship.

In the same way you can pick up a lot of information by how someone feels to you. It really is the same gut feelings and knowing with meeting a new spirit. To me meeting spirit people feels no different than meeting a new friend. Spirits will also use feelings to impress you with their messages of love and feelings of how proud they are of their loved one. I also feel in my body the area that may have been hurt or injured so that I may learn how they passed on or what they were physically struggling with when here. We tend to discount our feelings but in the world of mediumship every feeling is a clue and a message so pay careful attention to what you know and feel.

Practicing getting in touch with your feelings and your senses helps to fine tune your radio with the spirit world. Practice when seeing a friend and tune into your feelings and ask your angel mentor to help you feel into this person's energy. Many people in the helping professions are natural empaths feeling other people feelings knowing how others feel very quickly. They can tell what another person is feeling because when they are close to them they feel their feelings. Being empathic is tuning in in the same way you would to speak to a loved one in spirit. When meeting someone new practice feeling into their energy how do they feel? We are all connected so when you extend your energy further out you can get very good at picking up what is in that persons energy field. This is why sometimes when you think about someone you are close with they call you within a day or two, they picked up your thoughts from your energy. When you thought about your friend, your energy extended out to them and they picked up on, Janice is thinking about me, let me call her. They pick it up with a thought or feeling about you. One day, I was worried about my daughter Noelle, she had walked into town with her friends. She didn't have her phone and I kept thinking Noelle come home now. I kept saying it over and over and within seven minutes she was walking up the path to our house.

 Try it, think about someone you are close with or talk to them and see if they end up calling or texting you.

It's fun to practice extending your energy to our friends. Sometimes when you feel into someone's energy you will get a quick headache or feel anxiety or worry if that is what they are experiencing. It happens to me all the time in my sessions. A client will come in and then all of a sudden I feel sick, come to find out that my client had been feeling sick. The impression doesn't last long, just a couple of seconds when you realize it's not you and the feeling fades.

Try feeling into your animal's energy and see if you feel anything. It can be really fun! My daughter who rides horses is always asking me how all the horses at her barn are feeling especially her horse, "Neeko". It surprises me that I feel different things from horse to horse. They each have a different feel to me and when I describe what I feel she usually says yes that's his personally or I can see him being like that. Some horses feel like babies, some teenagers and some very irritable and grouchy just like us on a bad day! Since developing my language my ability to feel has dramatically increased. I used to not be as affected by my feelings. Now they are very strong and hard to ignore. But it's a small price to pay to be able to help people and animals. It makes sense that tuning into your senses will make you even more sensitive than you already are. Rate on the scale of 1-10 how is this clair for you? Does it feel stronger or weaker than clairvoyance? Record your answer in your journal.

Clairgustance

This clair is the least common but when you experience it really surprises you. I remember doing a reading and I was talking to this woman's grandfather and all of a sudden I smelled cherry tobacco. I was so surprised! It was so fun to smell something that wasn't here. In another reading I smelled apple pie, it smelled so real. I actually walked into my kitchen because I thought someone must be making apple pie. Some mediums have this as their strong sense but most people on occasion have a clairgustance experience. Practice by remembering what your favorite foods smell and taste like, apple pies, brownies or cookies. Remember the smell of the summer air, the beach. Just recall as many of your favorite smells as you can to practice. Ask your angel mentor to give you something to smell or taste. Practice! Again, rate this clair. Was this easy or hard for you on the scale of 1-10 and record it in your journal.

All together now

It's time to now put all your clairs together! This is basically what you do when you do a reading. You use each sense to connect with spirits. Take a peach and hold the image in your mind. See the peach clearly. Now how does this peach feel in your hand? What is the texture? Now hear the word peach in your mind. Next taste the peach what does it taste like to you? In this exercise you just used each of your senses just like you would in a reading! Easy right? Keep practicing and make sure you see, hear, feel and taste. Practice with an apple or any other food or fruit.

Next try people. See your best friend, hear her name and sense how she/he is feeling today. Does a smell or taste come in related to your friend? Try people that you know are in spirit and recall them, see them ask them to give you a message and hear something from them. Get a sense of a message for you or how they are doing. Try one of your pets either here or past in spirit and go through each sense. Really practice the more you do when you are doing a reading it is easy and you know how to talk through your senses because you are so familiar with doing it.

Strengthening

This is so exciting you are learning how to communicate through your senses! Now you want to work on strengthening them so your connection is strong and your readings are more accurate. The first exercise I want you to try is the traffic light.

Picture a traffic light in your mind and hold it for a few seconds. Now I want you to see the green light and hold the green light in your mind for one minute. Now I want you to go to the yellow and do the same. Then red, make sure you are holding this image as least for a minute and if you can do more that is great. If you want you can add any color you would like the greater amount of colors the better.

If you are really motivated, go on to practice the other clairs. How does the green light feel to you? Hold that feeling for as long as you can. Green to me feels cool fresh and feels to have a lot of depth to it. That's just how green feels to me. It may feel very different to you. There are no wrong answers as this is practice. Then hear the word green and hold the word in your mind as long as you can. If green had a taste what would it be and hold that taste. Do this for yellow and red.

This is valuable because when you get an image from spirit it comes in very quickly and leaves quickly. You have to be able to go back into your memory and hold it so you can look at it again. When a spirit gives me a picture of themselves, I have to hold the image so I can make out all the features. The stronger the better this practice makes it easier to hold and report to your sitter what you are seeing.

It also helps to clear your mind out. When you are holding the green light in your mind you are not thinking other thoughts just in the same way you do in a reading. You are receiving, holding and reporting the information.

The subject of your practice can be anything. Pick numbers hold the number five in your mind for at least a minute then go to ten and so on. Try shapes; hold a square in your mind, then a circle, triangle and so on. Hold a yellow circle in your mind and then add a green triangle in the circle then put the circle in a red box and hold it. This type of practice strengthens your ability to hold your connection to the angels and spirit people as well. When you are speaking to a spirit and giving validation and messages you do not want to lose your connection. The connection is like tuning to a radio station you don't want static on it (your thoughts) or lose the station completely (your connection.)

The Blossoming of the Clairs

The angels shared with me that your clairs; how you see, hear and feel spirit does take time to develop fully. Of course that isn't what we want to hear. We want to connect with spirit immediately, like yesterday! Trust that the angels will help they have the perfect curriculum for you.

The angels showed me a rose blossoming and said "We can't rush this rose can we?" No we can't, but we can give ourselves what we need so we will thrive and bloom when each of us is ready!

Have patience with yourself, the angels and spirit. Opening up takes allowing on our part and not rushing or forcing. In time, you will be fluent in this language and then you will look back and say, "I should have just relaxed and enjoyed the process." It doesn't matter how young or old you are your clairs blossom in the time they need. Lean on the angels and your angel mentor. Relax into their love, safety and guidance. They will never fail you.

An Angels Touch

When you are meditating or talking to your angel mentor you may start to notice what I call, "an angel's touch." You could feel a change in the air; it may become cooler or you feel a patch of warm air. You may feel tingling in your hands or fingers or by your head. Maybe you hear a slight whisper in your ear or a touch to your face. Notice what you feel this is your angel's touch! You will notice because it usually is the same feeling or experience whenever they are around. Guides also make their presence known in the same way. I have a guide that when he is around he will whisper in my right ear. I know my angels are around when I hear and feel a vibration. I have also experienced my angels putting their warm vibration on my hand to comfort me. The energy is warm, loving and reassuring.

During one of your meditations ask your angel to come to you and notice any changes or feelings you get. Then ask your angel to step away and feel how it feels when they leave your energy. Then ask them to return and feel again what they feel like when they are close by. What you feel is their touch for you. It is special and unique as you are. Keep trying until you know what they feel like.

Do the same exercise with your guide. If you don't know who your guide is ask who is around guiding you. Ask for a name and feel what your guide is; a male or female? Do you see them? What do they look like? Write down immediately what you get so you don't second-guess yourself. My guide Jon had been in my dreams for as long as I can remember as a loving presence. Waking up after those dreams, I felt so loved and not alone. I knew they were more than a dream because these dreams didn't fade like many do. Now I see him clairvoyantly as he is always there to give support, love and direction. We all have guides and angels around us so use your "clairs" to get to know each. To start, ask for one guide you don't want to confuse yourself with too many energies. After a while you will be able to tell the difference between a guide, spirit and an angel. There can be slight differences but as your clairsentience develops your ability to feel energies will also. At this point, if you are a beginner you are just at the beginning of learning to talk through your "clairs" so have patience for yourself and realize this takes time and commitment. Like anything, we need to learn and as we do to be loving and unconditional with ourselves. Don't let your doubts or fears stop you from connecting to your friends in spirit. They are rooting for you and want so much for

you to learn so that you can have all there
love and support.

Vibration Time

This is a big factor in your being able to connect to the world of spirit. Spirit lives in the vibrations of love, appreciation and gratitude. They have very high vibrations and it's easier for us to connect with them when we are at a high vibration. I always noticed that when I fell in love my abilities where at their highest. It took me a while to make the connection but it was there. Being in love with someone or loving your life and others is a blessing and a gift. This is why meditation helps too because like exercise, meditation raises your vibration naturally. This is where the angels really assist us because we need to see our good and highlight all the time, how wonderful we are which helps us to keep our vibration high! They always talk to me about helping others be more forgiving and accepting of them. The angels only see our good and nothing else and they want us to do the same. When we treat ourselves like our own best friend it's easier to stay happy! WE just can't afford to be mean and negative and then expect to connect with these beautiful high vibrations. It's good motivation to be nice to you along with a high vibration you also manifest the things you want in your life, two really great motivators to work on your mood.

Keep track of your mood for one week to raise your vibration. If your mood is below a five you have some work to do! Keeping your vibration high, which is the key to manifesting.

Vibration Exercise

Circle the number that represents your mood in the morning, afternoon and evening. (one is a bad mood and ten is the best mood ever!)

Copy the next page and track where your mood is throughout the day. Once your mood becomes the focus you can see where in a day your vibration takes a dip. When doing a reading you want to make sure your vibration is at least a five and try to get it higher.

Monday-

1   2   3   4   5   6   7   8   9   10

Tuesday-

1   2   3   4   5   6   7   8   9   10

Wednesday-

1   2   3   4   5   6   7   8   9   10

Thursday-

1   2   3   4   5   6   7   8   9   10

Friday-

1   2   3   4   5   6   7   8   9   10

If you find you are at a five or over, great job! If not time to get to working! Your vibration affects your connection to spirit so get Happy!!

- Play a game to see how high can you get you mood to go
- Write down things you are grateful for
- Think of funny memories or stories or shows
- Think of past accomplishments, things that made you feel great
- Look at beautiful pictures or go outside in nature
- Write a new story of how you want your life to go.

- See yourself in the future you so desire.
- Think how lucky you are to be you
- What favorite words or phrases make you feel good?
- Meditate

Write down some of your own:

_____

_____

_____

_____

_____

_____

_____

_____

_____

_____

_____

_____

_____

_____

The gift

The angels wanted me to talk to you about this concept of people having gifts or being gifted especially in the psychic and mediumship arena. They want you to know that you are the gift. They point out that there is a danger idolizing people or granting them the title of being part of a chosen few, the gifted. The angels want to level this playing field for you. We are all special and unique and how we live our gift out is our choice. What we create is up to us and when we see ourselves this way there is no stopping us. Part of living our gift out is just to follow our natural interests and desires and if you have an interest and a desire for mediumship, then you will connect beautifully.

The only requirement that you need to live your gift is your own support, encouragement and permission. You are special enough, smart enough, and good enough to do anything you have an interest or desire to do. Gifted people as we call them, did one beautiful thing; they gave themselves permission to allow their greatness to emerge and so can you! We each have such different desires and there are plenty to go around so you don't ever have to worry about a shortage of them.

In mediumship how you speak to your angels and guides and spirit will be different and special because you are the channel. Each of us channels in our own special way and that gets expressed and delivered with our own unique stamp. The angels want you to feed this interest you have with encouragement, support and patience. They can only do for you what you allow so please don't take this opportunity away from you by feeding any doubts or fears that you may have about learning mediumship. If you have the desire you have the ability and if it's not coming instantly that doesn't mean it won't. The angels are giving me a guarantee that you can and will do this. Just give yourself permission to grow and develop into all you desire and the angels will to be right by your side cheering you on!

Symbolic Language of spirit~

Symbols are a common way the angels and spirit communicate with us. To me it sometimes feels like I am learning a new type of sign language. Spirit people live in a different vibration than we typically do. Our vibration is lower and earth bound, where they are of a high energy and frequency. These differences can make talking a challenge. Think about how easy it is to miscommunicate with someone in the same room as you! Think of the game telephone and how easy it is for messages to get distorted person to person. This is why spirit works so hard to give us symbols that make sense to our clients and us.

Symbols work nicely because one symbol can mean so many things to your client. Like for example I saw a rose for my client and her mothers name was Rose but she also loved roses. For this mother this was a perfect symbol.

In your journal keep a separate space for your symbol definitions. You might get a symbol that you don't know what it means till your client explains it to you. Like during one reading, I was talking to my client's brother who passed when he was a teenager. I saw a letter in an envelope so I was asking my client had she received an important letter recently or did she have a letter she was keeping from her brother. She said no she didn't remember getting any special letter and she didn't have a letter from him. I didn't recall seeing a letter like this before so I wasn't sure what it meant. Her brother had been talking about her son so I asked trying to make sense of the symbol. I asked "Did your son get a letter recently" and then it hit her! "Oh my!" she said, she had received an email yesterday that he got a special award. I laughed realizing the mail I was seeing was email. I thought that was clever of her brother. How else could he get me to email?

It is really hard to talk in symbols. Think of how would you identify yourself through symbols to your loved one? It's a lot harder than we think so make sure you and your client really explore each possibility.

Think about some common symbols and if a spirit gave you one, what would you think it meant? What if you got a flag or a school? What do you think the spirit was trying to tell you? There could be many meanings. If your clairsentience is strong you can feel into the symbol to see if you can feel what it means or whom it belongs to. Like with the school. When I saw it I wasn't sure who or what it belonged to, but then I felt mom and job. My client's mom had been a teacher. Some mediums will at that point just say was your mom a teacher and some mediums always give the exact symbol. Like they may say, I am seeing a school and it feels like it's connected to your mom in some way like maybe was she a teacher. Both ways are fine it is up to you, but I like to give everything I am seeing just in case they can make more sense of the symbol than me. Practice getting symbols by asking spirit to give you one now, what did you get? Write it down in your journal.

Symbols also can move I have seen flying planes and balloons floating so keep that in mind. Also if you get a symbol that doesn't make sense to you or your client, ask the spirit to give you another or ask if they can be clearer. Many times I have to ask spirit to make things clearer or bigger or to add more. It seems when spirits are talking to us they give us the information and they don't realize that sometimes the information either didn't come through, or it's too fuzzy to see. The spirits are busy giving us information, but they don't know how we receive it so we have to let them know when something is unclear, or we don't understand what they are saying. They are happy to clear things up but you have to let them know, just like you would if you were having a conversation with someone here. If you were unclear, you would say I didn't understand what you just said. It's the same in the spirit world.

Questions to ask spirit people

1. **Gender male or female**- You may either see or feel the gender or hear who is with you. If you see the spirit, then you can tell quickly if it's a male or female. If you feel the spirit you will be able to start to tell male energy vs. female energy. If you are getting male and your client says "no" you can ask did your mom have masculine energy? Just check in case they could have been very non-traditional and that may make sense.

2. **Relationship**- If you sense a female, but not sure of relationship your next question is what is the relationship, mom, sister, etc.

to this person. The relationship you usually feel or hear the words Mom or sister. Always double check. Sometimes I will feel older brother and they will say, no younger, but he actually always acted like the older one. Remember they retain the same energy there as they did here.

3. **Age passed**- Ask when passed. I see a timeline in my mind by decades so I get a sense of age and I don't look to be exact. Start at ages under ten, then teens, then young adults, middle age, or above. Spirits now give me the range. I will feel forties or fifties etc. When you look to be too exact it can cause your reading to go bad. If you start hearing "no", that affects you and your

client so staying a little general with some things is fine. If you can get specific that's great. If you get 35 you can say did this spirit pass around 35 and they will either say exactly or close, they were 38. Sticking with did they pass around an age is helpful.

4. **How passed**- Was it an accident, tragedy or illness. Ask the spirit to use your body or see an image of a body in front of you to feel or see what part of their body was affected. Do you feel or see something in your *Upper body*; head, chest, heart, lungs or *lower body*; stomach, liver, bladder, legs.

Look up an internal body part picture online. Go over major organs and where they are, so when you feel a spirit pointing to that area, you know what they are referring to. I sometimes hear "liver" or feel something in my chest. It can vary spirit to spirit on how they give me this information. Just when you get comfortable getting information one way, they like to change it up. They like to keep us learning and growing.

5. **Names or Initials**- When getting names from spirit it's a good idea to give your client three choices of similar sounding names or just give initials. If you say I have a spirit Diane here and, if it isn't the right name your client will start shutting down. Always give your client choices even if you hear the name clear as a bell. Unless every

time you get a name you are right. Give choices like it sounds like a D name like Diana, Diane or Dan. This way your client searches for the right name instead of saying no and stops thinking of people in spirit. You will get other information to verify it's that person, so you don't want to get stuck. I have gotten the name wrong but then got eight more pieces of right information validating this person and my client is still stuck on the name. They may say "but her name isn't Diane it's Denise". Help your clients to not get stuck by offering choices.

6. **Physical traits**- When looking for appearance, ask for highlights what were

they known for; hair, complexion, smile, eyes, etc. Everyone has a standout feature. Many spirits if they were good looking will tell me they were. They may tell you funny things like distort their nose, so you know to say did they have a funny nose or a big nose. Spirits over exaggerate to get your attention! Just tell your client what you are getting. They will know.

7. **Physical illnesses**- Chronic problems like diabetics, knee problem, arthritis, headaches, etc. These are illnesses that they didn't pass from, just what they struggled with or were known for. I might see spirits holding their heads for headaches, or sitting in a wheelchair, or

see a cane. I might see a needle for drug use or diabetes. Remember there are many meanings to one symbol. Make sure you go over each, as it could be different with your client.

8. **Career**- There are many such as; homemaker, accountant, policeman, nurse, hairdresser, mechanic, etc. I love asking for a profession. Sometimes I just hear it, and sometimes I will see a things like a badge for a policeman, or a white nurse's outfit. I will see cars with the hood up for a mechanic. I sometimes see a spirit counting money for accountant.

9. **<u>Significant events</u>**- It's fun to get months or dates for birthdays, anniversaries or weddings. I will see cakes for birthday and numbers for significant months, or I will get the month. So I might see the number two which can mean February or I see the word February. Some mediums scan the months starting with January and go through each month and see what month the spirit stops you at. Again your language with spirit will be different than mine! You will find your own style, but these are just examples. Start by scanning the months so you tell the spirit to stop you at a significant one.

10. **Favorite pastimes**- Reading, writing, knitting, sports, etc. I will see a stack of books for reading. I will see knitting sticks for someone who knits. I will see jerseys with numbers for sports. I might see a baseball or a baseball cap or a bat. Many universal symbols with sports.

11. **Significant places**- Many spirits can take you to their homes, vacations homes and show you important items. You may see pictures on the wall, favorite rooms, etc. Ask a spirit to take you to a special room or their favorite painting.

12. **Types of food they liked or made**- Spirits may show you their favorite recipe

or have you smell their homemade apple pie. You might see a rolling pin or a mixer. If the spirit was a professional cook you may see a tall chef's hat.

13. **Types of clothes and jewelry**- Items that you may have from them or just their favorite pieces. Many times spirits come in their favorite clothes. Often I will see men in flannel shirts or suits if they like getting dressed up. One time I saw a woman dressed in men's clothing. When I told my client she laughed and said "yes!" she dressed masculine. If your mom always wore shirts then she comes to me wearing a shirt. I often see jewelry floating before me.

14. **What are some important memories**-
Spirits have shown me them dancing or
playing the guitar or drums. They show me
boats and canoes if they liked boating.
They show me airplanes if they were big
into traveling.

15. **What pets did they have?**- When I
ask spirits about their pets I often see an
animal walking around or a cat in their
arms. And again, look at the sign language.
One spirit showed me them holding the
dog which meant to me this dog was small
enough to hold and was treated like a baby.

16. **<u>Where were they buried?</u>**- Many people are buried and will show you a gravestone. Some will show you other things like ashes being thrown into the water. If there is a special message on the grave they may show that to you. They may show you a plaque in memory of them or a special bench that was in their memory.

17. **<u>Show you scars and injuries or tattoos</u>**- Spirits will show me tattoos on their arm or legs. Sometimes I see the tattoo but sometimes I just see an outline of it. I might see a scar or birthmark and sometimes they just show me the side of the face that it is on.

18. **Show you signs they are still around**- The spirits will talk about births and deaths since their passing. Many spirit people tell me who is with them now, and that they are happy to be together again. They will talk about what the client is struggling with, as a way for them to see that they see what is currently going on with them.

19. **Show you a special memory to your client**- Spirits show me special trips, or going to a special place like a park, or the circus. A place that was special to my client. A young boy too young to speak when passed showed me ducks. His mother said

that's what they did daily before he passed they went to a special park and fed the ducks.

20. **Show you a special object**- I see necklaces, crosses, rosaries, plants, army dog tags, nameplates, rings, pearls, and religious items. Coffee cups for a lover of coffee. I often see trees that were planted in the spirits memory. I might see a letter being put into a casket or I the jacket of the person. I have seen cards and Mass cards from spirits.

21. **Have them drop a special object in your hand or put it on the table in front of you**- This is a great way to get the spirit

to put the item in your hand. When you ask, you will always get something. Don't be surprised. One time I got a clock the spirit wanted to tell my client it's time to move on and live again. This is such a fun way to get a symbol. Ask your angels to drop a special item in your hand and see what you get. What does it mean and what was your angel trying to tell you?

22. **Special message**- The special message should be last. You want to get as much evidence as possible that you have the person your sitter wants to connect with first. The message is usually loving and touching. Remember you are reuniting two people who have not

connected in this way for many years and you are the channel. But make it last piece of information so your client feels certain you have connected to their loved one. After the message, sometimes I feel my client getting upset because they know the reading is almost over. I always ask the spirit to give me a sign that they will use to say hi and send their love. I like to give my clients the connection to take with them so they don't feel this spirit is now gone. The spirit will give me a sign like pennies, feathers, phones, butterflies, birds, radio, TV or clocks. These are ways their loved one will stay connected. Later people will come back to me saying; "since your reading I see penny's all the time. Thank you. Now I know it's my mom".

This helps them to maintain their own ongoing connection. Many times when I tell someone what the sign is, they tell me yes, they see that sign all the time. They were just not sure it really was from their loved one. I love when this happens because you get another validation and the ongoing link for connection at the same time.

You can make your own list but remember to have validating information first then messages.

Receptive states

When are you the most receptive to see, feel and hear spirit? Can you guess?

Early in the morning just as you awake when you are speaking the language in your dreams and still have a vague memory of how to do it. The morning is also when you are in a slight altered state. This is the same state you are in when you do readings. Make a point before you go to bed to ask your angels or someone in spirit to give you a message before you wake up.

When are there other times? Many times throughout the day! Especially when your conscious mind is busy but relaxed. Like doing laundry, putting the dishes away or when you are taking a walk. I get many ideas for my books when I go for a walk. My mind and body are slightly busy but I am relaxed as I walk. This gives spirit and the angels the opportunity to send me inspiring thoughts and feelings. I am always writing ideas down in my iPhone on walks. During the shower is another time. Make it a habit and ask spirit and the angels a question every time you take a shower. Make a separate place in your journal for shower questions. Why is this so? Some say it's the ions in the water and some say you are relaxed and in that meditative state. Maybe it's both, I am not really sure but I do know it works! It even works to ask a question and then put your hands under running water. Many times I get messages when I am just staring at the television but not really watching it. Again in that altered state. Try taking a glass of water or fill a crystal bowl of water and stare through it. It's like looking into a crystal ball. It's the staring or zoning out that puts you in a receptive state. There are so many times during the day that we are naturally in this receptive state. So pay attention and ask your angels questions during those moments.

Message Delivery

When doing a reading it is so important to get into the habit of giving your messages in a way that does not shut down your sitter or yourself. When getting information from spirit, especially in the beginning there may be some confusion and misinterpretations on both parts. It is great when you get evidential information like if this spirit was male or female, and they passed from a heart attack, etc. The more on target the better. When you are first learning and even the more advanced medium should always keep in mind to deliver messages that help your sitter to search for answers and not shut down. The messages and symbols you get from spirit are always correct but they may be misplaced onto the wrong spirit or your client has forgotten important information. Always give choices for interpretation. Like giving three names that sound alike instead of one that is wrong and then they stop thinking, "Who could this be?" Giving options and choices keeps your client engaged and active which keeps both of your vibrations high. When you are getting a lot of no's, both vibrations take a hit and it may be difficult for you to keep your link to the spirit world.

I was doing a reading for a woman and her friend came through. I kept getting someone had recently bought something big when they had gone shopping. I was asking her, "Did you recently buy something big?" She kept saying, "No!" I kept giving her choices because the message was so strong. I knew it wasn't wrong, but something was off. I asked her if her friend bought something big before she passed. She thought about it and finally she said, "No, but she was a really BIG shopper!" I started laughing. I had reversed the message. Instead of getting she was a big shopper, I received someone bought something big when they went shopping. We both cracked up!

Yet, giving her options prevented both of us from shutting down.

Many times my information is off so slightly and it can be missed. This can happen in less factual messages, It happens and in messages that you hear or feel. Those messages tend to be longer and there is more room for misinterpretation. Often I have to help my client figure out where the message fits. When I asked a few questions such as, "Could this belong to you or the spirit?" Together we usually can find it. The longer you do readings the better you will get at message delivery. It is a very important and often overlooked issue that can cause a reading to go in the wrong direction. I remember giving a Facebook reading and I asked if the spirit smoked because I smelled smoke. Her response was, "No." Then I asked if smoking was an issue for this spirit. She started to think and burst into laughter. She said "OMG" he hated that I smoked and I just went to light up a cigarette! If I hadn't kept asking we both could have missed such a funny message!

Remember that what you receive from spirit is never wrong! It can be misunderstood, unverifiable, but it is not wrong. When we start a reading from the point of that first message, no matter what your sitter says, you are not wrong. I love how John Edward always challenges the people he reads for. He is a good example of someone who always trusts spirit his connection and what he gets. He won't let a message go and will keep asking the client to search to make sense of the information. If he has to he will call other family members to help his struggling sitter. His faith in spirit and himself is very strong and that is how you want to be too. In the beginning, you may not trust yourself but you can always trust what you get from spirit. I am not as assertive as John. I receive and share messages in a more open dialogue. This is especially important as you are beginning to learn mediumship.

When you develop you will know what messages are factual for you that you can just present and the ones that need to be given in this way.

The clairsentient messages are the ones that you are at the most risk for misinterpreting, so pay close attention to those. Usually when you see and hear things, they are often accurate. In time, you will see where your accuracy lies and that is a big help. I know with names I often get the initials correct, but not the name. On occasion I do, but not all the time. Since I know this about myself, I always give choices. My dates, months and numbers are very accurate, so I can just present them. But messages that I have to interpret,

I give in this open-ended style so the sitter can help.

The Angels mean business

Taking money to help people always made me feel uneasy. Even in my psychotherapy practice I always had a hard time when it came to the money part. I felt guilty, like somehow making money in this way was wrong. This is absolutely not true!

It has taken me most of my career and the angel's help to see this differently. The angels' view of money is simple, money is another form of love. They know we need to provide for ourselves and they have no issue at all with us charging for our readings and making money. They love when we make money and feel happy and abundant! There is no issue in what makes us happy and comfortable. It makes them happy for us! They enjoy what we enjoy. There is nothing wrong with any form of abundance that is something we have learned here. They don't want us to devalue ourselves in any way and not charging proper fees is devaluing. There are standard fees for mediumship readings so find out in your area what they are and use them as a guide. Your time and energy and all you have devoted to learning your craft is valuable whether you are a beginner or an advanced medium. Ask the angels for help with this, especially if you are having a strong reaction to reading this section. All abundance is our natural right and when we allow it in, we can all have it. It is a worth issue for many of us. Am I really worth it? The angels answer is yes you are! Everyone can and should be abundant. Some people are just better at allowing it into their lives. The angels assure me there is enough abundance for us all.

I overheard some mediums talking about how they worry if they will have enough business. There is more than enough business for us all. Just like my psychotherapy business.

I used to get fearful that there were so many therapists and how will I have a full-time practice? Then I realized that I couldn't possibly see more than fifty clients a week. This would be true for other therapists as well. Many are needed in both professions.

Happily charge a fee for your readings and feel your angel's joy as you feel your abundance as they do too! The more money you allow in the love you are allowing into your life!

Come alive with the Angels

The angels are always reminding me in very loving ways to come alive! They want me to see more, experience more and have many more joyful experiences. I have a tendency to fight this! I will tell them, "I can't right now, I am a single mom of two teenagers and I need to work!". They patiently smile at me and push me to go for a walk and for some strange reason I cant get Pandora to work and I am forced to take in all the beauty that the Village of Port Jefferson has to offer. The sights and the sounds are beautiful and I get the point. There is always time even in my busy life to: see, hear and feel. I laugh to myself thinking I had to learn to connect with people who are in spirit to learn to come alive and enjoy my life! How ironic!

They tell me love myself and make me happy that's all there is to do and that's our job here. It's to fool around goof off and have fun! They say it's in those moments that you are fulfilled and happy! That's the big path we are all driving ourselves crazy to find? I think not! There has to be more? They tell me yes we like to grow and create and we get a deep satisfaction in doing that but we also need to enjoy our creations. We want to savior and enjoy them! When we go back to spirit we evaluate ourselves by asking one simple question; "How much fun did I have?". They say in spirit we savor each golden moment of fun and each beautiful experience one after the other. We don't punish ourselves and torture ourselves with mistakes we may have made. All the negatives beliefs we hold just vanish into air like it never happened.

They don't want us to ever punish ourselves now or in spirit. They say stop! Love yourself and like yourself today! Don't worry so much you are a beautiful spirit. Don't worry about your body so much it just holds your beautiful soul. They tell me to take good care of my body like I would anything I value but my body is not me. They suggest having a healthy regard for it but don't waste your time on it. Use your body as your vehicle to experience life here on earth but that's all. There is no need for a constant evaluation of it. They share with me that there is no need to hate your body so much! Whether it's young or old, thin or fat it makes no difference. The message is always the same. It's not you and who you are, let it go and go back to creating and enjoying your life! Don't wait to be thin or beautiful or wealthy to be happy, be happy now! Your spirit knows happiness, joy and that's all. Ask your spirit and the angels to help you come alive again. What does this have to do with mediumship? Everything! To connect with spirit all your senses have to become very sensitive to you and your life. This is how you grow your clairs. It's hard to explain but once you experience this beautiful awakening you will know!!

Before and after

Before a reading and after is when you need your angel mentor the most! Doing readings, especially in the beginning can be anxiety producing. It is not easy trusting in something that feels so new. This is where your angels come in. Ask them for help before your reading. Ask them to calm your nerves and to help you keep your ego out of it. What I mean when I talk about our "ego" is the unsupportive person that lives inside of you critiquing and criticizing everything you are doing!

Your angels will remind you that this is a natural language for you and you instinctively know how to link with a spirit and talk with them. You were once spirit and your body is a home for your spirit. The spirit inside of you knows exactly how to do this when you allow it.

Spirit-talk is normal and natural for you as talking to someone here! Ask the angels to remind you how to do it and then you are going to have to take the leap of faith and do it. Before readings, I would go for a walk or meditate if I was too anxious. Listening to my favorite music really helps because it helps to get you into a good state of mind and relaxes you. Do the things that feel good to you and ask the angels to help and give you some more ideas. They are very insightful and always come up with great ideas. They know you so well and they will put into your mind the perfect remedy. I laugh because my angels are always telling me to drink lemon water. It seems to be their cure all for me! What will they suggest to you?

After the reading you will feel a range of feelings depending on how well you think you did. Of course your angels are giving you a high five! However, the odds are you aren't. Ask the angels to help you to see the truth about the reading. That you are learning to connect is the most important thing and spirit sends you people that are perfect for your level. There is a reason the angels gave you this sitter and the reading may only be a small part of it. Know that you have something very special to give this person even if you feel like a beginner. Your energy and your love and connection will naturally help this person without you having to do anything. So rest assure you are always giving your sitter something very valuable and special just by connecting and trying. We don't know everything and we don't know what truly helps another. Perhaps this sitter was meant to be affected by your energy or your loving smile. Don't discount you even if you are a beginner. Trust the angels as they know who to send you and who you can help. When we think we have failed this is when we have been of great service!

If you feel good and it went well you are probably feeling quite high. After a good reading, I am giddy and sometime lightheaded from the vibration lift.

Make sure before, during and after you drink a lot of water, readings can dehydrate you. After the reading you want to have a nice grounded meal. Foods that grow in the earth are great for bringing you back to earth. Usually I barely eat before a reading. Afterwards I am starving and I then have a nice meal to ground me and I feel back to normal. I also like to go outside for a quick walk when I can. If you can't, don't worry!

Doing normal everyday activities helps to ground you again naturally. Ask your angels what foods are best for you. They will give you the thoughts and cravings for the perfect food.

Always remember that after the reading you should be proud of yourself no matter how you think it went! How many people take this kind of a risk to work with the angels and spirit? This is such important work and your desire to do so makes you very special to the angels and spirit people. You were led to this path for all the right reasons. Now you just have to work on letting yourself shine!!! Think about the first time you learned anything. It's not an easy process yet in the end, it was worth it. See yourself as a happy learner, you are learning now and forever on this magical journey. It is normal to make mistakes and not be perfect. We don't yell at our children when they are learning to walk. We help them when they stumble and fall and you and your angels will do the same for you. Have faith in them and have faith in you. Take good care of your body and spirit before during and after each reading. Have fun as the angels aren't that serious and what us to laugh easily and enjoy this process more.

I know I can get very serious about it all and they remind me lighten up and laugh. It is not easy when the people you read for come with sadness in their hearts. We are to be a reminder that their loved ones are alive as ever in spirit and still a big part of our lives. The spirits don't want us to see them as gone but in a very active and vital part of their loved ones lives. Reading after reading you will see how they want us to get that message across.

They are not gone, just in spirit! You will feel who they were here and even see them with their old body. Many times the spirits like to come at the age they felt they looked best at. It always makes me laugh but I would do the same! So remember, many times they will show you themselves at a younger age.

This is a never-ending beautiful language as we are eternal and we will always speak it. When we each return into spirit it continues and we become fluent once again! So, don't get impatient with yourself. You have all the time you need.

Happy connecting!
Sending you all my angel Love-
Janice Mary

EXERCISES

These exercises were taken from my online course <u>Angelic Mediumship & Mentoring Program</u>. Try and do one exercise a day to develop and strengthen your skills.

Let's Talk Lemon Water~ Angel Tip for the day

The angels reminded me today to talk to you guys about lemon water. We need a lot of water connecting to spirit. Make sure you drink as much water as you can and if you like lemon all the better. The angels always tell me let people know, drink lemon water it's like their cure all. Hot, warm or cold it doesn't matter just drink away and be happy.

Significant Month

Ask your angel mentor for a significant month connected to a friend or someone you work with. Write out the months of the year. Scan the list and see which month you stopped at. You can also ask for a month and see what one comes into your mind. Write down the first one and try two more times. Sometimes the first thing we get can be from our thinking mind and we want to receive the message.

Yes Or No Questions

Ask your angel mentor a yes or no question and see how the answers feel. Do you hear it or do you see it? How do you get a yes? What color is your yes? How does no feel? Do you see a color or feel something in your body? Do you hear no or do you see no floating in the air? Practice all day today asking questions that you get a yes or no. Write down your experience in your journal.

Male or female energy

Getting to know the difference between male and female energy for you is very helpful. How you sense, hear or see the difference will help you to determine the sex of your spirit client. Practice noticing how does female feel to me, how does male feel to me. Be mindful of all the people you will interact with today. Write down what you feel, sense or hear. How many men? How many woman? Write down how many of each. Again this is just practice to help you get very familiar with how the difference for you feels. It is very different for each of us. Did you notice how we each got different information for the yes or no questions? It might be slight difference but it is there. Have fun with this and write in your journal the difference for you between male and female

Clairsentience

We are all energy even though we are in a body. Just like a table even though it seems solid is filled with energy. We are all connected, so it is easy to see how simple it is to feel the energy around us. Practice extending out your energy and feeling into another persons or even an animal. Think of a friend today and extend out and see if you start to feel anything different. Think about someone close to you today and ask them to call you or text you over and over in your mind and see if they do!!! I love feeling into the energy of my daughters horse and her friends horses they all each have a distinct feeling and personality! Keep it simple and have fun.

Focus

Take a blank sheet of white paper and tape it to the wall or your computer screen. Relax and focus then ask your angel mentor to come in and give you information. Again this is to get used to how spirit speaks to you and where it comes from. Look at the paper and see what you hear, feel and see. Use this paper as your spirit movie screen. Ask for names of people who are around you. Keep your focus and no thinking or judging what you are getting. Let the information come in and just write it down as quick as you get it. Relax and have fun.

Names

It's great to get names so lets practice seeing and hearing names. There is no right or wrong just practice in how spirit-talk comes to you. Relax for a few minutes and ask your angel mentor to give you a name relating to a friend or family member. It's helpful to see, if are you getting the initials or the full name. This is very common for even the most advanced medium so don't get frustrated with yourself. This is the beginning practice of sorting out what is your thinking mind and what is receptive spirit-talk. Ask in the shower or run your hands under water experiment and have fun.

Visualize

Try and visualize your angel mentor giving you each piece of information for the spirit that comes to you. Your angel mentor hands you a slip of paper with information on it and sometimes it's very clear and sometimes it looks like it is in a different language. You do your best as a medium to make sense of it. But what is clear is that you and your angel mentor are never wrong but things can get lost in translation. Trust your angel mentor and trust you to do the best you can knowing it will continue to get better and better.

A Gift *(A short Meditation)*

Take a few deep breaths, relax and follow your breath for a minute or two. Imagine yourself walking into a light pink mist. Feel this sparkly pink mist around you. Relax for a moment and then look to your left to see your angel mentor. Feel your mentors love and excitement to see you again. Your angel has a gift for you, it is a beautiful leather bound book. Take this book.

This book is warm and glowing and you feel the warmth go through your hand and down your entire body. It is healing and relaxing. This book looks oddly familiar to you and you feel so much gratitude toward your angel to have it. As you look through the pages you notice the written words are foreign yet familiar.

This book is all about you. It is your book of knowledge filled with nothing but joy and gratitude for who you are! Take this gift with you and symbolically place it somewhere in your home. When you look at it you will remember who you are, your spirit and your home. It will help you to connect to your spiritual home while you are here. Take this beautiful book as a connection to all the love and appreciation they feel for you.

Beam of White Light

(A Short Visualization exercise)

Your angel mentor is going to send down a
beam of white healing light that completely
surrounds you!! This beam of white light is
filled with love. The light funnels down, it is
your channel to them and the spirit world.
Let this white light wash away any fear or
doubt. Allow the messages to flow down
this funnel from your angel. What do you
hear, feel or sense? Let your angel remind
you how to speak to them. Feel your own
spirit and connect once again to your home.

Take with you the feeling of love, support and gratitude for who you are and all you do to help others. Your angel knows and loves you and sees how hard you work and how hard you try. Let your angel make it easy for you. Let go and allow them to teach you! All you have to do is be an open channel to receive.

Psychometry

Psychometry is when you perceive intuitive symbols from an object that belongs to another person. It tells us a story about the person who owned it. Take an object from someone who has passed into spirit and hold it in your hand. Notice what you feel, hear, see and maybe even smell or taste. Write down everything you get. Ask for memories of this person's life. Pay attention to any impressions you get in your body. You can even ask a friend to give you an article or piece of jewelry from someone special to them who is now in spirit.

Clairvoyance & Clairsentience

Grab a box of crayons and take out the main colors. Put them in a bag, close your eyes and pull out a crayon. Ask your angel mentor to show you what color crayon you are holding. (keeping your eyes closed) Ask three times for this color. Sometimes the first color you see can be from your thinking mind. To prevent this ask three times for each color and notice how the one that is correct comes into your mind.

The next part of this exercise you will do the same as above but this time feel the color. What does this color feel like is it cold, cool or warm? Write down all you feel relating to each color in your journal. Have fun with color.

Waking Up Our Senses

The angels have taught me that to connect with them and spirit we have to become more sensitive and alive! Pretty ironic but true! How does this painting make you feel? Write down all your impressions in your journal. Do you hear anything feel or see anything from your angel mentor about this famous painting?

Clairvoyance Time

This exercise is meant for you and a friend (that likes jellybeans). What color jellybean is their favorite? What is the first color that comes into your mind? What color do you see in your minds eye?

Card Readings

Do a simple three card spread for a friend or yourself. Pick your favorite deck! Ask your angel mentor to bring a spirit friend to you. Ask three simple questions from your list and write them down.

Heaven's gate - A meditation

Taken from my first book "The Forgotten Friend"

Here's a guided meditation that I felt inspired to write and I wanted to share it with you! Just tape it with your iPhone in your voice, which makes the meditation even more powerful. Take a moment to go on this spiritual journey, and see you through the eyes of love-god-source.

Let's take a walk to heaven in your mind. We walk together in a gentle, peaceful way. I am with you, as well as anyone else you might like to invite along, God, your guardian angel, a family member, a special pet, anyone who comes to mind, who puts you at ease, makes you feel safe, secure and protected as we travel.

We now walk together with our companions by our side, and you will begin to feel the warmth of the sun shining down on your face. With every step you take, you feel the sun's golden rays on each part of your body from your face, to your neck, your chest, your stomach, legs and your feet. The warmth of this sun seeps into every cell of your body, relaxing it.

This special sun has magical properties that heal any physical pain your body may have, or any emotional pain you may be dealing with. Let the sun's rays absorb any burdens, worries, or pain.

With each step you take, you go deeper into this relaxed state of healing. Now I want you to look over to your right and see the path we are approaching. It is nestled in the most beautiful place you can imagine. There are warm streams and bustling wildlife around you. The scents of lavender and roses hit you immediately and you don't even have to be close to the flowers to smell them. You notice the colors of these flowers. They are the most vivid blues, purples, and reds that you have ever seen. They come alive in their vibrancy.

The sounds you hear, you can also feel. They are the most beautiful sounds you have ever heard. The running of water, the birds singing. You can actually feel the sounds running through your body.

We finally come to the end of the path, to an old ornate gate, and you see a heavy chain and lock on it. It's the gate to your heaven. Look at the lock, it looks strong and heavy. The chain that wraps around the gate, and keeps it closed, has many links on it. Each link symbolizes a belief you hold about yourself, and the heavy lock holds the limits you have placed on your life.

Look away for a moment and then look back at the lock. The chain has disappeared right before your eyes, as well as the beliefs and limitations you hold. They are self-imposed and have little meaning. The gate is now free to open to your heaven.

We walk in, and you see all your dreams and your wishes. Everything you ever wanted to become, everything you ever wanted to have, and everything you ever wanted to do or see, is here. Look around for a moment and take this all in.

As we continue, we come across two mirrors, one filled with cracks and chips, and one standing beautiful and tall and flawless.

Stand before the cracked mirror. This is the mirror and the refection you have created. Each crack represents your thoughts about yourself, every attack, every criticism. Every time you treat yourself in an unkind way, a crack appears. This mirror is so marred with cracks; you can no longer see your reflection. All you see are the cracks reflecting back.

Now, come look into God's mirror. Do you see any cracks? There are none. Look at your refection in this mirror. You can see yourself reflecting brightly. This mirror is flawless, and so are you. You can see your spirit—your true self. You see your beauty, the real you.

You can't hide yourself, your soul, your spirit, in this mirror. This is your true reflection, not the cracked one you created.

Take a minute and just look. You can ask yourself, your spirit, any questions about your life, and see and speak to the real you. What do you need to hear? See? Feel? Spend a few minutes with your accurate reflection. Let God show you and tell you the truth about you, no matter how beautiful it is.

It's time to leave, but you are leaving without your burdens and without your faulty beliefs. With each step, you are filled with renewed joy for the path you will create for yourself.

Take your heaven with you, and leave all your limitations at the gate. They have already disappeared.

Open your eyes, feeling more alive, feeling lighter, brighter, healed and free. Take with you, your true reflection.

This meditation was taken from my first book "The Forgotten Friend" by Janice Fuchs

Multi-Clair Development

Take a deck of playing cards and place them face down. Pick up one card and then feel, hear or see where the match may be. Pay attention to how your angel mentor is talking to you. Have fun with this and you can't get it wrong. Ask to be pulled in the direction of the match. You can match by number, color, or suit. Have fun.

The Meaning of Roses

Roses are an easy symbol for your angel mentor and spirit to give you. Ask your angel mentor to hand you a rose now. What color is it and what does it mean to you?

You can ask spirit to give you roses as a symbol for a loving relationship, a marriage, an anniversary and so on. Write down what each color rose means to you and watch spirit use roses to communicate with you. A blue rose may mean a recent passing, however you can assign whatever meaning feels correct for you. A red rose with obvious thorns may mean a loving but painful or difficult relationship. If Roses speak to you use them to help your mentor quickly and easily communicate.

Make a splash

Ask your angel mentor for a color. What did you receive? Write down everything you feel and get regarding this color. What does it feel like? What message does this color have for you today? Is this a happy color or sad color? If you have dye take a glass of water and put in a few drops of this color. Stare at the water for a few minutes. Relax and ask your angel for messages. What do you hear and feel. Write down everything and anything that comes into your mind no matter how small. This is how you learn to trust what you are getting from spirit and your angel mentor. Have fun and post your experience.

Hearing & Feelings Names

Grab a bowl and put in slips of paper with different names written on them. Write as many as you would like. Mix them up and after meditating or relaxing ask your spirit mentor to help you feel the difference in the vibration of names. Each name carries its unique vibration and it helps to feel and hear them together. See if you get the entire name correct or it's initial.

For The Sitter

When a student is doing a reading for you remember how it feels. We are all so sensitive and doing readings in the beginning can make us feel very vulnerable. When giving your feedback don't say "no" instead say "I will have to think about that or I am not sure at this moment". No can shut your reader down and the link they have with your spirit family so just be sensitive to that.

For The Medium

When giving readings remember there is only love in spirit and the messages will be supportive and loving. In the beginning as we are developing it is important not to give advice or interpretations of the information you are getting. When you get a symbol first give the symbol and let your sitter figure out what it may mean. It is always better to give exactly what you are seeing and help your sitter with the meaning.

It's important for you to have your own standards.

1. Can my messages be verifiable?

2. Does the information give hope, love and support?

3. Does this information empower the person I am reading?

Exercises taken from Janice Mary's angelic mediumship and mentoring online course.

If you are interested in taking this course you can find it on www.angelpractitoners.com or contact Janice Mary at janicemart40@yahoo.com

www.ingramcontent.com/pod-product-compliance
Lightning Source LLC
Chambersburg PA
CBHW052009090426
42741CB00008B/1611